# CREATE YOUR BEST YEAR ONE DAY AT A TIME

A Peaceful, Poetic Inspiration
Guide to What You Want
the Most This Year

Clara Angelina Diaz

Library of Congress Control Number:        2017914495
ISBN:            Hardcover            978-1-5434-5145-0
                 Softcover            978-1-5434-5146-7
                 eBook                978-1-5434-5147-4

Print information available on the last page.

Rev. date: 10/24/2017

To order additional copies of this book, contact:
Xlibris
1-888-795-4274
www.Xlibris.com
Orders@Xlibris.com
767643

## Dedication

*To my daughter Angelina
and to all the daughters of the world:
may you find your own way and formula for creating
the best years of your life.*

To: Brenda

To Your Vision & Dreams!

Love,

1/6/2018

# Contents

# 1

# The Birth of this Book

*"Grow where you are"*
-Clara Angelina Diaz

**I**t was during a long, cold winter that my mother, my three siblings and I immigrated to the United States from the Dominican Republic. I was eight years old at the time, but did not feel like a child because I was the eldest of the four.

As far back as I can remember, I have never felt my age, and have been very aware of having a rich and creative imagination. Long before we arrived in the United States, I had been nurturing fantasies of how amazing my life would be in this new country. I imagined that we as a family would be so happy, that the streets of the United States would glitter with gold, and that I would have my own bedroom with shiny white furniture, and curtains and a matching duvet on my bed.

The reality was very, very different. We arrived in Manhattan in a cold, dreary October. The streets of New York City did not glitter; instead, they were just cold and gray. We didn't have a big castle like I imagined; my siblings and I all shared a very small bedroom in my father's uncle's house. Adjusting to this new country was a struggle for me. Being the oldest, I had to learn the English language as fast as I could to help myself, my siblings and even my parents navigate our new reality.

My father struggled to find meaningful employment, and needless to say, life got very stressful for us as both parents tried to find work. We ended up moving to Massachusetts, where we lived in a government shelter for six months. Eventually, we were given government-subsidized housing in Boston.

As the years went by, I started noticing that I would get really sad around the same time every year. I did not know there was a name for this: depression. I just thought my hatred for the cold was the cause of my unhappiness. I didn't know that there was more to my annual cycle of sadness. When I became more self-aware and embarked on a personal development and spiritual journey, I realized that the connection to my annual dark times coincided with when my family and I first arrived from the Dominican Republic. I realized that those difficult times still lived within me, and that every year through spells of depression I was unconsciously living out the feeling of uncertainty that comes from moving to a whole new country.

I decided that I no longer wanted to live a life full of sorrow and sadness, and started making conscious efforts to have more positive experiences—especially during this time of year. I started measuring my progress in life by counting my blessings and successes, and began feeling a little better and more confident each winter.

As my inner strength grew, I challenged myself to make not only the *winters* amazing, but to make each *year* the best it could be, for me. I was already practicing living in the **now,** through my discovery of the book *The Power of Now* by Eckart Tolle. I decided to start making the year I was in the best year of my life by making each *day* the best I possibly could. I made a conscious decision to do everything I could to create my best year, and made personal development a priority.

That is how this book was born. It began with a need to share the tools and practices I adopted to improve my own life and maintain a positive state of mind throughout the year. Not only did I want to share those tools with others, but also—and more importantly—I wanted to share the amazing way I was now able to feel, by exercising my power of choice.

# We Are Here

We are here,
   You and I, ready . . .
      Ready for love and change and progress and more.
We are here wishing
      Wanting
         Desiring
            For something to be added to our existence
               Or taken away.
Ready.
   Allowing the miracle of life,
      The natural flow that gives rhythm to life.
Manifest the good.
Clear away, make space for new things.
We are ready.
Growing pains, sweaty hands,
Afraid of the new and letting go . . .
                           It's part of the process.
Do this as fast or slowly as you can
And if you think you can't,
   Have compassion for yourself
      And encouragement
         In place of the fear and doubtful voices,
Because at the end of the day
   Your life is expressed like the roses—
      Beautiful,
         Always timely,
            Loved and protected, always!

# 2

# Peaceful Purposeful Progress

*"Everything comes to those who live in peace and clear purpose"*
—Clara Angelina Diaz

I always considered myself a "make-it-happen" kind of person. Being that way served me well for a long time. Somehow I have always managed to get more done than the people around me. That's all fine and dandy when you're a single woman who has all the time in the world to just do, do, do.

It was having my daughter that transformed me. Before she was born I had grandiose ideas of how I was going to run my business while she napped—and also be a full-time, stay-at-home mom as well.

I've never been so wrong in my life! With my new baby as the center of my world, I could no longer make things happen like I once dreamed I could. I was feeling pretty frustrated one day with all that was expected of me as a new mother and an entrepreneur. One day while nursing her, I asked myself how I could keep my centering intention to enjoy being a mother and also continue working on my dream: building a business that empowers women to live from their core values and exercise genuine power and confidence.

It was right then and there, lying on my side with my baby girl, that I heard these three powerful words: *"Peaceful purposeful progress."* These three words lit me up like a lightbulb! These words are like a calming song that I now sing to myself and the women I work with in my journey as a new mother and an entrepreneur. Every day I tell myself that I will make peaceful, purposeful progress, as opposed to pushy, random reactions to getting what I want, from fear of not getting it.

**Peaceful:** in the way that I approach myself, my activities, the relationships I have with the people in my life and with my clients. This peace allows me to come from a place of abundance, where what I want is already manifested as I walk confidently in the direction of what I desire. With this peace I allow space for miracles to occur, as I am open to receive them.

**Purposeful:** in the way that I invest my energy, with clarity of purpose and intention, recognizing that every moment is an opportunity to live and act on purpose.

**Progress:** acknowledging what I intend to make progress on, and also knowing that any detour can also be progress in the direction of learning. Remembering that Life carries me.

These three words are at the center of my work every day, and help me stay on target. I hope they will do the same for you.

# A Declaration to Kick-start Your Year

*Your year starts when you say it starts.*
*You don't need permission to hit "Restart"—*
*not with abandon, but with intelligence and heart.*
*You, my love, deserve a second chance,*
*a third, fourth, fifth . . . seventh chance!*
*This is your year, this is your time.*
*Own it, shape it, make it into what you want*
*and make this the Very Best Year of your life thus far,*
*because you know what . . .*
*next year and the year after that,*
*you'll do it all over again,*
*but with more power, more intent.*
*And each and every year will be a little sweeter,*
*or maybe a whole lot sweeter.*

*So stay with me on this journey*
*of self-expression and maximum creation*
*of the very, very, very best years of your life—*
*one day at a time!*
*Yes, there will be bumpy roads, rain,*
*and who knows what. . . .*
*But I guarantee you this:*
*follow the words in this book and*
*you will set yourself back on the path of light*
*and happy creation of your very own life!*

# 3

# The Intention of this Book

*"Always start with a clear intention, it determines
the quality of your manifestation"*
-Clara Angelina Diaz

This is a daily motivational book to help you achieve what you want most in life, while feeling good about yourself and feeling peaceful about your whole life.

I believe the best way to create the life you dream of is by focusing on living every day in the best possible way you can, with all the resources you have. If a day-by-day approach feels too much at times, a moment-to-moment approach works too. I encourage you to make every moment count, and exercise your power of choice to achieve your dreams.

My story is one you can hopefully learn from and derive inspiration from. For many years I kept falling into the trap of setting huge goals for myself. I found myself either falling short of or not attaining the goals in some way, because I didn't have the knowledge and tools I have now. Not reaching the goals I set for myself impacted my self-confidence and made me feel like a failure, because as a high achiever I wanted to hit the mark every single time.

One of the major goals of my life was being able to finish college. It took me over ten years to do this, but I finally did. I would not take back that journey. Through the completion of this goal I have become a more persistent and patient person.

As I was completing my degree, I started my coaching practice. By writing my final thesis on how coaching can improve the chances of entrepreneurial success, I was able to merge the launching of my business with the completion of my degree.

In the research I did to both start my business and complete my thesis, I found that I wasn't alone in wanting to reach my full potential, and in feeling like I was not good enough to create the things I wanted in my life. I found that millions of people all across the globe felt this way, especially women feeling torn between fulfilling their responsibilities and following their dreams and passions.

This book is my attempt to share some of what I have learned in my own path of spiritual awakening, along with some of my academic research and also what I have seen in the lives of the clients I serve. At my core I have always known that there had to be a different path to feeling fulfilled and to achieving one's own definition of success.

All of this led me to finding a different way of living my own life and measuring my success. I made a decision to have only positive thoughts about the activities in my life. I decided to trust the universe that I was supported and worthy of what I desired in all areas of my life, and decided to simply live one day at a time.

My goal was to make every single day the best day of my life. This goal, although it sounds simple, is not always easy, but the decision is powerful. It was by breaking down my daily activities into small steps and doing my best in meeting those daily targets that things started to change for me.

I went through a self-discovery process that helped me achieve my goals each day, and in this book I will take you step by step through that process. I will share with you some of my personal prayers, poems and affirmations that I use daily to align with the best parts of myself and make the most of every day. I will also share with you stories of women in my own life who have made decisions to transform their lives by living in their truth and purpose.

As a life and business coach, I am especially passionate about empowering women and girls to exercise self-leadership, self-love and self-confidence in order to uplift the world with their unique gifts. Everyone has unique gifts that can be expressed in many different ways, and each person can kick-start positive changes in their lives and help change society by using these gifts. I am here to help you accept this about yourself, and to assist you in finding a definite purpose for your life.

My desire for this book is that you are inspired to create your own way and formula for creating the best days of *your* life.

# Encouragement

*How far can one*
*Go, go, go,*
*With a little encouragement*
*Toward the light, the right, the true, for*
*you? Be the light—you are the light that*
*transcends The dimension of time*
*Because*
*I light, you light, love.*
*We are capable of that. Encouragement:*
*give it with love and prudence To yourself*
*towards the light, Towards others,*
*And always*
*Peace, love in courage.*
*Go on, encourage!*

# 4

# Start Where You Are:
# The Power of Clarity

*"Clarity is not always necessary to take the next step,*
*but it gives a turbo boost to the necessary courage"*
-Clara Angelina Diaz

I know what I want and I am going to get it." "I want to go there." "I want what she has." "I have no idea what I want." "I just don't know what to do next."

All of these statements are excellent starting points on the path to clarity. The truth is that the conditions or the timing will likely never be perfect or right. So just start.

Feeling uncertain? This is the beauty of beginning: whatever you think you are moving towards transforms in the most beautiful way by your taking action—any action. The more inspired, conscious and courageous your steps, the more powerful your results will be. And of course, baby steps count.

Begin where you are, with what you have, and watch what happens. Do it as an experiment, or do it as if your whole life depends on it. Do whatever works to move you in the direction you want to go.

Start where you are, because you are worth having what you want, point blank. You are an amazing being and a brilliant soul who came into this world as an integral part of this interconnected web of energies we call life. Listen to the calling of your spirit that says, "Begin!" Make the call, say yes, say no; you know what you must do.

Do not allow the ghost of uncertainty to overpower your courage. Just start where you are. Miracles will happen, especially if you wake up every day with the renewed faith and conviction to start again where you are, building on what you have already done. And even better if you are working with a beginner's mind.

This year, this day you can start again where you are, as many times as you need to. Give yourself the permission and the support to start again and again.

You can use the Wheel of Life exercise (Chapter 8) to help you get centered. Remember what you are choosing to create, and allow your heart to speak to you, telling you how you can start again.

# In Her Own Words

## Start from Where You Are
Latonia Francois

**H**ow do you find strength in a dark place to overcome what seems impossible? Before starting my blog, "Let's Write Life," my life was lost in tangles of sadness that imprisoned me from believing I could ever overcome the challenges I faced. At that time in my life I was dealing with broken relationships, rejection from people I loved, and was pregnant with my second daughter. Stress during my pregnancy caused me to be out of work and financial issues began to take a toll on my ability to support my family. As a result of all the issues that surrounded me, I hit rock bottom and fell into a place of depression where I had found myself too many times before.

Ironically, this time rock bottom was the very place I was when I found the strength to never let depression, broken relationships, fear, rejection, my past, my doubts, my worries, or the hurtful opinions of others steal my joy anymore. I was tired of it all. My only desire was to be happy.

Journaling has always been a meaningful part of my life. It has been the only way I've known how to express myself in good times or bad. I had no idea what it meant for me to "be happy," but I made a decision in 2013 to begin a journey through journaling to discover what it meant, and to overcome my silent struggle with depression that imprisoned me for years. That journey led me to discover joy, spiritual awakening, the power of my words, life transformation, and a new level of loving who I am in ways I never thought could happen for me. That journey—which started from such a dark place in my life with no money, no one I felt I could reach out to, no real plan, and a baby on the way—became the very journey that changed my life and marked the start of a path that launched "Let's Write Life"!

Just when it seems like you have taken all the pressure you can take, that is the moment you realize you are strong enough to do the impossible—even when everything seems too far out of reach! Start from where you are. Have faith. Pick up your pen, become the author of your life, and let the power of your words lead the way! Your life may never be the same. It happened for me. I pray the same blessings happen for you!

You may contact Latonia Francois at:

www.LetsWriteLife.com

# A Poem for Today

*Dear Today,*
*Thank you for being here!*
*No, really, thank you.*
*I know sometimes I neglect you.*
*I think of yesterday so much*
*and of tomorrow too often,*
*but today,*
*Today, I only think of you*
*and I thank you for always being here,*
*oh, so faithful,*
*waiting for me every day, Today.*
*Thank you.*

# What can I do today to make this the best year of my life?

_____

_____

_____

_____

_____

_____

_____

# 5

# Define Your Best Year

*"Don't count your days; make your days count."*
—Anonymous

So how do you create your best year? How do you create an amazing, fascinating, happy, exciting, fulfilling, productive and successful year? This question must be running through your mind as you prepare to change the trajectory of your life. The short answer is to **define it.**

You start by creating a clear picture of what your ideal year will look like. Develop a mental picture of the future you want to create. This is crucial, because if you don't know what your destination looks like before you start taking steps toward it, you will not recognize it when you get there. Worse, every-where will look like your destination, and it will become easier for you to lose track of what you are aiming for. By defining what your best year will look like, you are also giving yourself something to look forward to—something that inspires you. And since inspiration is one of the most potent forces in the world, the picture of your dream year will keep you going, even in the face of challenges that will eventually come.

Imagine ending your day saying, "Today was a great day and I feel amazing about it"? Wouldn't you love to have lots of those days where you feel really good about yourself, your life and everything in it? I am talking about days when you accom-plished all that you wanted to do. Days when you go passion-ately after your goals and you achieve each and every one of them, with a clear and life-affirming intention in mind, knowing exactly why you were doing what you were doing. Can you imagine days like that? Days when you pay attention to life and life just flows. While days like this may sound surreal, the reality is that you *can* create days like this on a frequently. Creating days like this requires planning, intentional action and compassionate discipline.

Take a minute and close your eyes. Take a deep breath and imagine you are on the most amazing vacation of your life, and at the same time you are fulfilling your life's most important goals. Imagine that! That's the kind of life I want for *you!* In order to have this life of uncommon success, however, you have to *intentionally* create it. I will show you how.

**Exercise: Visualizing Your Best Year**

Creating the life of your dreams requires alignment to what you want, faith, effort, discipline and intentional action. Most importantly, it requires you to be aligned with what you want. To help you achieve your goals and create the life you desire, answer the following questions. The level of honesty that you express during this exercise will determine to a large extent whether or not you will eventually be able to create The Best Year of Your Life.

**What does my best year look like?**

**How does my best year feel?**

**What am I already doing to create the best year of my life?**

**What habits can I let go of to have the best year of my life?**

What am I willing to do right now to start creating my best year?

Who can support me in creating my best year?

What do I need to do to keep myself motivated in pursuing my best year?

# In Her Own Words

## Becoming Your Own Best
## Friend and Coach
### Linda Gonzalez

Loving yourself well is a fundamental act that engages the cosmos in your well-being. It first requires acknowledging that you are a worthy endeavor and then it requires being who you are. We are born with the belief in our worthiness: babies and little children insist on the value of their needs and the right to have them met.

Slowly we are hit with "adultism," the societally accepted norm that gives adults the right to denounce and diminish our human child rights. With that as a backdrop, we cannot be surprised at how poorly we have treated ourselves.

This "adultism" is a secret—not visible or discussed. We have it bred into us, like a hazing process that we then turn around an inflict on others. Think about how many times you meet people and don't bother to introduce yourself to the children. Why not? We have internalized the lack of impor-tance of children. Such a loss. As adults, we should be giving children the basic respect of saying, "I see you and you are valuable, worthy, and capable at any age of being my teacher, my companion and my inspiration." I recently found a picture of myself as a child in which the joy of my being shines through. If that kind of photo is not possible for you, then a picture of a child you love can be your guiding star.

To love myself well I continually look for signs of my immense heart, mind and spirit. That requires me to see myself reflected in the beauty of the world. First and foremost I notice what is available in each moment to soothe and warm my soul: the autumn leaves turning into the colors of a sunset, people offering love to follow my dreams, music that inspires me to sing and dance, and daily gratitudes that remind me that the universe supports my friendship with myself. I developed the habit of kissing myself, especially on the top of my shoulder, when I am in bed. It is a sweet and simple way to remember that I am my best friend, no matter what has occurred that day. During the day I am looking for ways that the world and I can "kiss" so that I don't look for this from people who struggle with their own worthiness.

I had to go deep into the foundations of my life in order to heal: finding the mold, the rot, the cracks, the exposed wires of my childhood and young adulthood. I named and rejected comments like "Children are to be seen and not heard," "You don't need to know why, just do as I say," "Your attitude is too uppity" and "You are stupid, good for nothing, a burra." With that work done, I began to breathe and access what I knew as a little girl. When something hurts, it hurts. When I am mad, I am mad. When I cry, there is always a source of sadness that matters to me. When I laugh, I am delighted. When I insist, something important is motivating me. I looked at where I was robbed of my belief that my needs mattered, and now say with my adult power, "I respect and value my needs."

Loyalty is a double-edged sword. I have been too loyal to people and organizations, to my detriment—trying too hard and for too long to be seen and have my gifts utilized. I am now loyal to my values and well-being. If a person or organization allows me to contribute my talents and receive respect and opportunity, then my inner coach smiles and I am all in.

Instead of being caught in the nets of other people's needs, I became the healing I had sought from the external world. I became my best friend and coach, constantly reminding myself of what I require to live with an open heart, mind and spirit.

Allow yourself to receive
what you want this year!

# My Love Gift to You

*Unlimited amounts of encouragement*
*Towards what feels good and true,*
*Laser-focus clarity to remember*
*That what you seek—it's seeking you,*
*And it's in the here and now.*
*Love energy,*
*Enthusiasm,*
*A constant reminder of your true identity,*
*The light core and power of life itself,*
*Which lives in you and around you.*
*Reminders of gentle pushes*
*Towards your mission*
*And your purpose.*
*You, in your heart, you know what that is.*
*Power in simplicity*
*And difficulty in matters where you forget to trust*
*And be clear on the definite purpose.*
*And in all this,*
*Remembering that all roads lead to God,*
*To love, to your purpose here.*
*You decide—yes, you!*
*You decide how much you will consciously enjoy it,*
*Day by day*
*And year by year,*
*Moment to moment.*

# 6

# SMART
# Goal-Setting Formula

*"The victory of success is half-won when one gains
the habit of setting and achieving goals."*
—Og Mandino

If you had to select *one* goal to work on this year what
would it be? One goal—just one goal whose importance is more
than the rest of your goals combined. Most of us have lists of
goals that we have carried from year to year, without even
coming close to achieving them. Sometimes we simply carry
them safely in our hearts and minds.

Right now I want to give you permission to give yourself a
break. Honor your desires and decide what goal you want to
manifest in your life this year. For example, I have decided that
my major goal this year is to publish this book, in both English
and Spanish, before my next birthday. This commitment keeps
me going even when I don't feel like it.

To accomplish your most important goal you must first
identify it, then decide to do your very best to achieve it—no
matter what obstacles and challenges life throws at you. You can
do your best, which may look different every day.

Once you have decided what that goal is, I want you to say
it out loud. Saying it out loud helps you communicate to your
subconscious; hearing yourself say what you plan to do gives you
a boost towards actually fulfilling that goal.

It is also important that you engage in positive affirmations concerning your goal, so that you begin attracting positive influences and forces that will further propel you towards achieving it.

Set your goal, commit to it, start taking actions, and speak it into reality. Let the universe hear what it is that you want this year. Let the universe feel the pulse of your desire. Let it feel the fire that burns within you, and witness as things start working together to ensure that you reach the goal you are so passionate about.

Now, in the space below, write down your major goal for this year. Write about how you will feel when you achieve it. Pour your heart out on paper, and let your words drive you to the finish line.

## My Major Goal This Year

_____

_____

_____

_____

_____

_____

_____

_____

_____

_____

_____

_____

One of the most important factors in determining the success of your goals is that you make them SMART. What I mean by SMART is this:

Specific
Measurable
Attainable
Realistic or Relevant
Time-specific

The goal that you set needs to have all these components. First, it needs to be **specific**. Any goal that is not specific is nothing but a wish. Instead of saying, "I plan to get in shape," say, "I am going to start exercising for thirty days, thirty minutes a day from 6:00-6:30 am so I can be more fit." That is a specific goal. By being specific you are able to determine the exact things you need to do to achieve your goal, eliminating vagueness and ambiguity.

Your goal needs to be **measurable**. How will you measure your progress? How will you know you are getting closer to your goal? It needs to be something that you can attain, but also something that's going to stretch you a little bit, or even push you out of your comfort zone. Imagine that you plan to write a book, and you set a goal to "write every day." Now, while that may be specific, it is not really measurable. If instead you say, "I will write five pages every day for the next month," it becomes measurable. That means every day you wake up and you write five pages, no matter what the weather might be, whatever mood you might be in, or whatever the circumstance may be. Every day you write five pages. If you get off track and write less than five pages, you get yourself back on track again the next day.

Your goal must also be something that is **attainable** and **realistic** or **relevant** to your life. It's a gift to yourself. You may be ready to take on the world after reading this book and feel like setting audacious goals you may never achieve, but you need to be realistic about what you choose for your goal.

If your goal is to start a business, write a book, attain a certain qualification, live a healthier lifestyle or get a new job, make sure that it is a realistic goal for *you*.

Finally, you're going to set a date so that your goal will be **time-specific.** Together we're setting date for a year from now. Whatever the day is that you're reading this book, just set a date one year from today. This will give you a target to shoot for, a time by which you will have reached your goal. Think about what you need to do within that year to reach your goal and plan out your steps. If you are truly committed to your heart's desire, you will achieve your goal.

The hardest part is always getting clarity on exactly what you want, why you want it and when you want it. By gaining clarity, you are better able to channel your mental and physical energies to ensure you achieve your goal. What is that goal? What is that goal that you have been putting to the side for years, that you don't believe that you can achieve? This year you finally will. You're giving yourself permission to go after it. You can do this!

Now write down your goal again and say it out loud in a positive statement. Declare to the universe and to yourself your specific, measurable, attainable-yet-pushes-you-outside-your-comfort-zone, realistic and relevant, as-a-gift-to-your-life goal.

# My Goal for This Year

Specific
Measurable
Attainable
Reasonable
Time-specific

_____

_____

_____

_____

_____

_____

_____

_____

_____

_____

_____

_____

_____

_____

_____

_____

_____

_____

_____

_____

_____

_____

# In Her Own Words

## Making Choices not Goals
### Nicole Moreno-Deinzer

At thirty-one, I have the luxury of looking back at my youth with fresh eyes to see the common threads of my thirty-one years of existence. We all have certain personality traits from childhood that have stuck with us and led us to where we stand today.

One trait that has woven itself around me each year is my "try it" attitude. In middle school and high school, I tried out for everything: track, dance, yearbook, band, field hockey, softball, cheerleading, choir, color guard, etc. Why? Because I wanted to. They all seemed like fun activities. I had friends in all of them. However, I quit most of them after two weeks or so. Why? Because I didn't love them. I tried them, enjoyed them, realized I didn't love them and let them go. Why waste my time and the time of others on things I didn't love?

The two things that I stuck with were yearbook and choir. I started choir in the sixth grade and yearbook in the seventh. When I love something, I stick with it. I made the choice to try new things. I didn't make it a goal to become "the best cheerleader ever;" even at fifteen I realized that was a ridiculous goal because that statement is so vague. Who defines "best"? What is the "best"?

Now fast-forward to my early twenties. I met my now husband, Nicholas. I didn't make it a goal to marry him. I didn't make it a goal to get married at all during that time, to my mother's disapproval. (Oh well, she still loves me!) I just wanted to have fun with cute guys. He just happened to be the cute guy for that weekend. After a few dates, a relationship grew, and eleven years later we are still together. I didn't set a goal to get married to him or to be with him forever. Currently our relationship goal is to be a strong support system for each other every day, and to voice our concerns if we don't feel that support. Everything else just falls into place. You see, at that age I made the choice to enjoy my sexuality, not a goal to be married by a certain age.

In my career, I made the choice to give up something that was making me miserable: working in the non-profit sector. I always enjoyed volunteering and giving back to the community, but I couldn't put up with working for the low pay and the lack of creativity in that job. I was being pushed into positions that I didn't like. What was keeping me was that I was working on community issues. I made a choice to leave, without any safety net. That wasn't the wisest choice, but I made it. No one else made it for me.

I decided to focus on school and build my online magazine, "Epifania." If I hadn't made the choice to leave the job that was making me miserable, I wouldn't have met Clara. I wouldn't have had the opportunity to be part of this book. I would have been spending years trying to make myself happy in in an unhappy situation.

Now, goal setting is a wonderful practice for me. I have, however, seen people set ridiculous goals that not even the American "royal family" (Jay-Z and Beyonce) could achieve. I use goal setting in both the immediate and also in the long-term sense. For example, it is my goal to get one hour of writing done today. That is an immediate, specific goal. My lifetime goal is to spend my senior years on a vineyard in Italy. All the choices I make in life are aimed to get me there.

As I enter my early thirties, I continue to make choices and not goals. I have a mantra that I use for life: "Read, write, meditate, travel, love." As long as I make time every week to read, write, meditate, travel and love, I will achieve my lifetime goal.

So stop beating yourself up and make the choice today to be happy. You deserve it.

Hugs and smiles,

Nicole

http://epifanialyl.com/

# Creating Realities

At the end of each day I feel so amazed
  About all the things I have been able to manifest:
    Opportunities, more joy, more money,
      Even more ease with saying No
        And joy in saying Yes.
Amazed. I am amazed!
Flutters of glistening blue light, from time to time I see . . .
An angel—a guardian it is!
These days I am so focused on the priorities of life,
  The ease, the faith,
    The grace that is consciously present in the flow of life,
      A constant desire for learning,
        A total acknowledgment of support,
          From forces and angels above and below.
Acknowledgement, as you know,
  Expands the presence of what is acknowledged.
This we know!
  More peace, more freedom,
    Direct asking and effortless receiving
      Is what life is about these days.
Doing less and achieving more,
  Giving more and living with less stuff,
    Cleansing all things, nooks, crannies and drawers.
This opens doors.
Abundance is a natural state.
At the end of each day I feel so amazed
  About everything I get to manifest
    Through acknowledgement of what I desire.
I, big I,
  Make and manifest.

# *What can I do today to make this the best year of my life?*

_____

_____

_____

_____

_____

_____

_____

# 7

# The Incredible Power
# of Affirmations

*"Affirmations are our mental vitamins, providing the*
*supplementary positive thoughts we need to balance the barrage*
*of negative events and thoughts we experience daily."*
—Tia Walker

It was through Louise Hay that I first came to know about
the amazing power of affirmations. I would listen to her hour-
long affirmation recordings day after day, and started to notice
that I felt much better and more calm. Positive affirma-tions, just
like negative ones, work. An affirmation is simply a thought or
belief that you continue to repeat to yourself. I used to have a
very negative, unconscious affirmation: "There is never enough
money." Because of this continuous affirmation, I hardly ever
had enough money. When I transformed this negative thought
into a positive one, "I accept and receive the abundance of
wealth you have for me today," the results were miraculous. It's
like having a conversation with the universe.

The two key elements of an affirmation are: first, formula-
ting the suggestion that you wish to program into your brain,
and second, the repetition of that thought. Affirmations are
powerful because they shape our lives, whether we believe it or
not. Have you ever had a friend who constantly complains about
everything in her life and says negative things about everyone
and everything? Have you noticed that she keeps attracting

these things into her life? The words you speak have the power to attract whatever it is you speak about.

Effective and transformational affirmations must:

1. State your intention for the future in the present tense,
2. Start with an "I" or "I am" statement,
3. Be positive.

Examples of positive, transformational affirmations: "I enjoy the freedom and finances to travel to a new vacation destina-tion each year" and "I love and accept myself just as I am.

Setting SMART goals will enable you to create the right set of affirmations to fit into your grand plan. Once you create and write down your affirmations, be consistent about repeating them until your subconscious accepts them and they become real in your life.

Repeat your affirmations at least three times a day: once when you first wake up, to remind you of what to gear your efforts toward; once around mid-day or after your lunch; and finally, before you go to sleep at night. After thirty days of repeating them three times a day, these affirmations will be part of the new thought pattern in your brain and a new positive habit for yourself. You will want to embed these thoughts more deeply in your mind until you reach the intention of each affirmation.

When you repeat your affirmations, it's best if you can take that time to focus on yourself and the goals you have for yourself, without outside distractions.

Here are some positive affirmations that you may use to create more positivity in your life. Choose the ones that most resonate with you, and repeat them three times every day.

I am present.

I am blessed.

I am made to shine.

I am a star.

I am the best thing that has ever happened to me.

I am a leader.

I am a powerful creator.

I have an amazing life.

I have the right to feel good.

I am wise and wonderful.

I can create my best year.

I can create my best day.

I can choose how I feel.

I can visualize my perfect future.

I can manifest my desires.

I am a direct creator of my life.

I am joy.

I am surrounded by abundance.

I align with my truth.

I allow myself to receive what I want.

I now stop worrying.

I know all things work in my favor.

I am loved.

I am protected.

I am energized.

I invest my time in positive actions.

I have power.

I am unstoppable!

I am creating the life of my dreams.

I am cherished.

I am wonderfully and beautifully made.

I am a direct creation of God.

And now, write your own affirmations. Include the specific things you want to see manifested in your own life.

_____

_____

_____

_____

# In Her Own Words

## Affirmations
### Christine L. Bowen

*"On average, we have between 50,000-70,000 thoughts per day, with 80% of those thoughts being negative in nature."*

**D**id that statement make you stop and think, too? And, guess what? Those thoughts you just had from the impact of that statement are in conjunction with those other thoughts running through your mind . . .

*This book . . .*
*Tonight's dinner . . .*
*Tomorrow's meeting . . .*
*The children's recital . . .*

Whatever the case, this is pretty much how thoughts run through our mind, all day, every day, as if on auto-pilot. Sadly, we have been conditioned to look at our circumstances through a negative lens. With thoughts that are negative in nature constantly running through our minds, could life then be an outcome of our thought process?

About ten years ago, my thinking was transformed when I partook in a 24-hour practice to observe and document my thoughts. No judgment, just observation. I was blown away to discover the number of things that ran through my mind from moment to moment. What was even more mind blowing was how many of those thoughts were negative in nature, and even derogatory.

My self-talk included statements like:

*"I'm such an idiot."*
*"Why can't I ever get ahead in life?"*
*"What's wrong with me?"*
*"I wish I wasn't so fat."*

Can you relate? It doesn't matter if it is the simplest of tasks or the most challenging circumstance, we beat ourselves up constantly for life not being the way we want it to be. This mindset also becomes a megaphone, amplifying the judgements of others and absorbing them into our identity.

This constant negative messaging sinks deeply into our psyche. With the passing of time, our self-esteem erodes to the point that our optimism is overshadowed by pessimism. Life becomes a burden, and hope seems like a fantasy. Eventually, we discover that life lacks meaning and purpose.

*As a man thinketh in his heart, so he is.*
*Proverbs 23:7*

The power to create our reality is a gift that many take for granted or aren't fully aware of. When we recognize that our reality starts with our thoughts, and we can create our reality based on taking actions driven by those thoughts, we can truly begin to live life on our own terms.

Yes, mindset matters with everything. If your current circumstance doesn't look like the way you envision it within your mind's eye, it's time to become more intentional with your thought process. We need to unlearn our stinking thinking and flood our minds with positive intentions.

Positive affirmations and self-talk are the foundation of a life well lived. Whatever we focus on expands. When we choose to start each day with positive intention, we immediately and literally create a better future for ourselves.

After my mind blowing discovery about how many thoughts run through our minds daily, I made a commitment to treat every single day like we do a new year. Greet the new day, express gratitude, and speak life into the things I want rather than the things I don't.

*Great Morning*
*Happy New Day*
*Today is the best day of my life.*
*This day will be a productive day.*

I also made a commitment to speak to myself as if I were speaking to someone I truly love. I call this process "courting yourself." Yes! Date yourself! We spend a lifetime courting other people, and it's about time we do the same with ourselves. This begins with how we speak to ourselves.

*I am positive.*
*I am powerful.*
*I am confident.*
*I am smart.*
*I am beautiful.*

What if all those positive thoughts you profess on January 1 you professed every day?

What if every day you could write the story of how your day will turn out?

What if. . . .

I invite you to give it a try. Create the reality you see in your mind's eye.

Create the masterpiece called your life.

# What can I do today to make this the best year of my life?

_____

_____

_____

_____

_____

_____

_____

# Raise Your Vibration!

*I learned to raise my vibration . . .*
*It happened on an early morning, Bright!*
*I learned to raise my vibration.*
*I learned to say, "Hi" to God.*
*When the outside world was too much to bear,*
*I blurred my vision to lower the Despair.*
*I closed my eyes,*
*I went inside, I made a bubble, I saw the future. I am ready.*
*I have the energy.*
*You have it, too.*
*Let's use it widely and wisely . . .*
*Let's use it now.*
*Are you ready to Shine?*
*Ready or not, come on!*
*Let's shine our lights,*
*Bright!*

# What can I do today to make this the best year of my life?

_____

_____

_____

_____

_____

_____

_____

# 8

# The Wheel of Life Exercise

*"When you see life as cyclical, manageable and evolving, you can prepare yourself for the next cycle with confidence."*
-Clara Angelina Diaz

I want to introduce you to the ultimate self-coaching tool—a tool I use with my clients to help them see their life from a bird's eye view, from a higher perspective. It's called the Wheel of Life.

What the Wheel of Life can do for you is help you to really take your life to the next level at any point . . . if you're doing a check-in maybe every six months, once a year, or if you just don't know what to do next. The Wheel of Life is amazing.

So all you're going to need is a pen or a pencil and this book, so that you can come back and check in with yourself in six months.

**Step 1.** Use the circle provided in this chapter; this circle is going to represent your life.

**Step 2.** The circle is divided into eight equal parts, for eight different areas of your life. Now label each part. Change the categories if you like, to fit your life better.
1. Health and Wellness
2. Money and Personal Finances
3. Hobbies and Recreation (things you do for fun)
4. Romantic Relationships
5. Physical Environment (where you are physically most of the time: everything from your car to your city, your bedroom, your house, your work space, your entire physical environment)

6. Spirituality and Personal Development
7. Career or Business (or Education, for those of you who are in school)
8. Relationships with Friends and Family

**Step 3.** Now close your eyes and take a deep breath, and think about this: How are you feeling about your life right now? How are you feeling about your entire life? Open your eyes, and looking at each section, rate each area from 0-10 with 10 being the best it's ever been.

**Step 4.** Decide which area you want to focus on. It doesn't have to be your lowest area; it could be one of your higher areas.

**Step 5.** Now really think about what would it look like if this area was a 10. How would you be feeling? What would you have differently? How would things be different if this area was a 10? Write that down in detail.

**Step 6.** The next step is to decide on one step, just *one* step that you can take today, this week, or this month—however long you want to focus on this area—to bring that area up to a 10. Again, write everything down in detail, as much as you can.

_____

_____

_____

_____

_____

_____

_____

_____

_____

_____

Now tell someone—someone who deserves to listen to you, to your dreams and your goals. Actually go and take that action. Go tell someone! And after you tell that person, then celebrate! Celebrate and give yourself something. Do something nice for yourself.

Then repeat these very same steps in all the areas of your life to create the Best Year of Your Life in each and every area. You can do this!

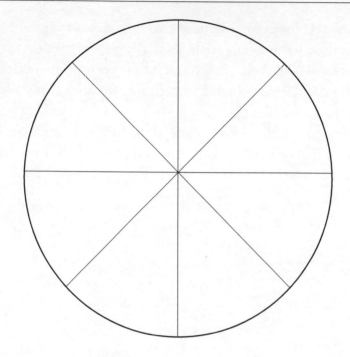

# The Wheel of Life

Label each section, then rate each section from 1-10.
Which area is causing you the most pain?

Which area is bringing you the most joy?

Which area do you want to focus on?

How do you want to feel about this area of your life?

What can you do every day to feel this way?

What is your true intention for this part of your life?

In your lowest-rated section, if it's not a zero, what is going right here?

Connect the dots representing your ratings. Note where the imbalances are.

# Soul Love

*Have you ever felt*
*Like someone was speaking to you and your mind,*
*Telling you to sometimes go left*
*Or right?*
*Have you ever thought about the fact*
*That you're guided*
*And protected*
*And loved*
*At all times?*

*It's not easy to explain,*
*But you are!*
*When Spirit speaks,*
*He usually has some very comforting words to say.*
*He says to me,*
*"Well, hello, my love.*
*Manifestation of joy and purpose are yours,*
*If you align with me,*
*Simply by remembering that I am you*
*And you are me."*
*Sometimes it's not easy to accept*
*That it is that simple.*
*Yes!*
*That you are free to express yourself!*

*That you have power to create your own way!*
*That you can make any change to your life*
*As it aligns with you feeling right.*
*That all great things are possible.*
*That they come to you one day at a time.*
*Knowing this, you can allow yourself*
*To release your fear of failure*
*As well as your fear of success*
*Because success is in the now.*
*It's in the amount of effort*
*That you are putting towards your dreams,*
*Your future,*
*Your idea of what the very best future for you will be.*
*"There is nothing to fear," says Spirit.*
*"Focus on your effort*
*And your results will come as a natural progression.*
*Keep going!*
*Trust me and you will see*
*One step at a time,*
*One day at a time,*
*With love,*
*One breath at a time,*
*With faith,*
*One action at a time.*
*Focus on this time, my dear.*
*You are guided at all times!"*

# 9

# A Love Letter from My Soul

*"Hey, Its your soul speaking and it says, wake up, I*
*need you, I want you. I am, you! Choose me!"*
-Danielle Laporte

**M**y first ever life coach gave me this amazing exercise during our coaching relationship. This was over ten years ago now. It turned out to be one of the most powerful tools I received from him. It's called a "Love Letter from the Soul." I want to share with you my own recent letter from my soul to myself, and invite you to write your own.

These are the instructions: go to a quiet place for at least an hour. Take a few deep breaths. Take at least three, although ten is better. Ask your soul what it wants to tell you, then write whatever comes into your mind. Let your hand just write.

Here is my letter:

## Love Letter from the Soul

*You are love, wonderfully made with joy.*
*You know that peace and freedom are your home.*
*That's where you are able to be your best—*
*Your best support, to yourself and others.*

*You are so aware of how valuable and loved you are.*
*You are in the full knowing of your purpose on this earth.*
*Through your talents and innate gifts,*

*you came to serve the world.*
*You are a natural communicator,*
*not just in one language but two.*
*A communicator of uplifting truth.*

*A voice for the voiceless, you are able to be a*
*medium through classes and cultures.*
*Yes, through classes and cultures.*
*You can speak to the children and the adults, too!*
*You can speak to the wealthy and those*
*who have forgotten their riches, too!*

*You know your place in this system of time and space.*
*You are a doer of good deeds.*
*You can stand up for truth, righteousness and justice,*
*Caring deeply about the way people treat each other,*
*how you treat others.*
*You care!*

*You know the little things matter and that the*
*richness of all is in the experience and the process*
*of what unfolds while arriving at the goal.*

*You can enjoy the process.*
*You know you are supported.*

# My Love Letter from the Soul

*Hi, It's your soul speaking . . .*

_____

_____

_____

_____

_____

_____

_____

_____

_____

_____

_____

_____

_____

_____

_____

_____

_____

_____

_____

_____

_____

_____

_____

_____

_____

_____

_____

_____

# Remembering
# What Is Possible

*I believe with all my heart,*
*and it is my desire to remind you,*
*that it is possible and attainable to be happy,*
*despite stress,*
*to be productive and learn*
*to manage your life with grace.*

*It is possible to define your ideal life*
*and confidently move towards it,*
*creating a life you love,*
*a life in the light.*

*It is possible to lead your life and business with love.*
*It is possible.*

*It is possible to be the leader of your present and future*
*and be the best version of yourself—now.*
*As your coach I will stand by you.*
*I will stand by your side*
*and with positive energy,*
*along with intelligent strategy,*
*compassion and practicality,*
*I will help you,*
*clarifying the way—your own way—one step at a time,*
*remembering what is possible.*

# *What can I do today to make this the best year of my life?*

_____

_____

_____

_____

_____

_____

_____

# 10

# The Power of
# Three Daily Actions

*"It happens in threes. Embrace the magic of taking three
important steps daily and surprise yourself with the results"*
-Clara Angelina Diaz

**I** want to introduce you to my little secret to creating your
best year—and your best day. I call it the Power of Three.
The Power of Three is simply thinking of three actions—three
powerful actions—that you can take today, *now*, to make it the
best day of your life.

Before we get into the details of the three steps, first really
think about how you want to feel at the end of your day. You're
going to plan your three actions around this feeling. You want
to feel good, of course, but think of a more specific word. Let's
create another word—beyond just good. Do you want to feeling
amazing, energized, empowered, courageous?

The word that I always go back to is *loving*. I want to feel
loving. I want to be loving towards myself, loving towards the
world, loving towards my life. And because I know I want to feel
loving, this allows me to think of steps I want to take throughout
the day that are loving towards my life. I want this loving energy
to be moving through my goals.

So, **first** think about Action #1. Think of the first action
you can take today to feel the way you want to feel. This can
be something that you've been avoiding. As one of my favorite
authors, Brian Tracy, says in his book, *Eat That Frog,* the action
you want to take first is an action that you've been putting off.
Start by writing, *"Today I will . . ."*

Action
#1:_____

_____

_____

_____

_____

The **second** step is to take an action that you've been *wanting* to take, something you really like to do.

Action
#2:_____

_____

_____

_____

_____

The **third** step is a *leap* action—something that you know is going to take you to another level. You know in your heart what that is.

Action
#3:_____

_____

_____

_____

_____

If you wish to have your best year, take these three steps *every* day: one that you have been avoiding, one that you actually want to take, and one that will take you up to the next level. Trust your heart, and take those three kinds of actions *every single day*. This is my secret to creating the best year of your life, one day at a time.

# Stop What You Are Doing

*Stop whatever you are doing . . .*
       *It doesn't matter where you are.*
*Snap your fingers twice*
       *And say the following to yourself,*
              *In a sigh . . .*
                     *"Remember*
                            *The True You . . ."*
*Take a breath . . .*
       *Express the fruits of your Spirit;*
*This is your only Truth.*

              *Deeply.*
                     *Go ahead and feel your lungs.*
*Go on and say:*
   *Peaceful, trusting, confident,*
       *Patient, loving, supportive,*
              *Wealthy, healthy, respectful,*
              *I am.*
                     *I am.*
                            *I am!*

# 11

# The Importance of
# Feeling Good about Yourself

*"The foundation of all success is that we feel deserving, and we can only feel deserving when we feel good about ourselves."*
—Clara Angelina Diaz

**I** want to share some keys with you, some key tips about how to feel good about yourself. As a couple of my favorite authors, Esther and Jerry Hicks, from their book, *Ask and It Is Given*, relate the wisdom of Abraham, "There is nothing more important than that you feel good."

I want you to start by imagining what *feeling good* looks like to you. To me, feeling good creates an image of being in front of the ocean, or on top of a mountain after a long hike on a beautiful day. So I ask you, what does *feeling good* look like to you?

_____

_____

_____

_____

_____

_____

_____

_____

_____

As a baby you intuitively knew that there was nothing more important to you than just feeling good. You were provided with everything you needed: food, care, shelter. This was all given to you. Along with the sun, fresh air and a life of possibilities, your life was very simple then. You knew what you deserved, and the world provided.

Somewhere along the journey of life someone told you otherwise, or made you feel that you did not deserve what you wanted. Fast-forward into the present: you start to notice that something's missing, that you don't feel good, and that the things that were supposed to make you feel good just don't make you feel good any-more. If you start to feel like you don't know where to go next, and confusion has kicked in, and if you're feeling just a bit unhappy with the person you have become, I want to tell you that this is a *good* thing, because you are awakening. You are awakening to knowing that you deserve to feel good, and to the truth about yourself.

To change from not feeling good to feeling good again, I have some tips for you. As an adult, you now have the gift of making life easier for yourself, and you can live in a more conscious way through the freedom of choice that life provides you. The need to feel good, in its simplest form, has been one of the most important guiding forces of life. We go to great lengths to first survive the elements and then to achieve greater heights to essentially keep having this "feel good" effect. As adults, it's extremely important that we feel good about ourselves, because feeling good about ourselves affects *everything* that we consciously allow into our lives.

When you look in the mirror, what do you feel about yourself? Do you love and accept the person you see in the mirror? Or, do you judge yourself and put yourself down? And if you're one of those people who feels good and loves yourself just the way you are, I congratulate you! I motivate you and invite you to help someone else get to that state. In order to get yourself to a place of *really* feeling good, here are some tips.

**Tip #1:** Define *what is going right* with your life. Literally, count your blessings. Make a list of twelve things that are going right in your life right now.

1. _____
2. _____
3. _____
4. _____
5. _____
6. _____
7. _____
8. _____
9. _____
10. _____
11. _____
12. _____

**Tip #2:** Consider the fact that *you can love yourself unconditionally.* Only you know what that means. Right now, think about twelve things you can do to love yourself unconditionally. These could be things like getting eight hours of sleep, or actually eating three meals, or simply taking the time to relax and take a deep breath. What can you do to love yourself unconditionally? Give yourself permission to do these things.

1. _____
2. _____
3. _____
4. _____
5. _____
6. _____
7. _____
8. _____
9. _____
10. _____

11. _____
12. _____

Now you need to commit your life to what's most important to *you*. Decide what you will give in your life. Plan your goals around what *you* want to give and what *you* want to do. With peace of mind, really think about what *you* want to experience in your day. Promise yourself that every day you will give focused energy, with love, towards what you want to create.

In order to feel good about yourself, you must first love yourself unconditionally. Be honest with yourself. Look at yourself with compassion. Define what's going right for you, count your blessings, and commit to what's important to *you*.

# In Her Own Words

## Trust Yourself, God and the Universe
### Massiel P. Eversley

At an early age I knew I wanted to make my family proud, have a broad, positive impact on other, and simply "do big things." Having my mother's example, I knew that hard work was required, and in order to accomplish "big things," you must operate outside of your comfort zone. After moving to the US at the age of six from the Dominican Republic, I learned quick lessons about the society we live in. As a female, immigrant, English language learner, daughter of strict parents, and a middle child, many things became clear. I knew there were rules that were in place for reasons bigger than myself, and I would have to learn to operate within these systems in order to be successful at anything I did. Still, deep inside, I knew that despite limitations it didn't mean the world wasn't my play-ground. So I felt every right to make reality the big sand castle I imagined on this playground.

I thought my life's roadmap led to a career in psychology. Once I entered college and was deep in my studies, I knew I was wrong. Being wrong is okay, but having time to do some-thing about it is actually great. I quickly reflected on how my mother was fulfilled by working in healthcare. Knowing that time waits for no one, I rapidly changed schools and majored in nursing. It was a spur of the moment decision. All I knew was that nursing had given my mother a joyful sandcastle, and I wanted one very similar to it. Changing the whole course of my life's direction was a risk. But to me, the biggest risk is the one not taken. This opportunity would only be my reality if I went and knocked on the door.

As I went on my journey I would always seek unique opportunities that made me stand out from the others. If the sheep went left, I always went right. I became a sponge and took in the wisdom of my mentors. But most importantly, I listened to my inner self. That is how I ended up as a nurse with a legal degree.

Many thought I was wasting my time with a non-nursing degree, but I tuned out the negative oppositions, reminded myself that I deserved the best and continued to manifest my dreams. I became a director after only seven years in my field. As I reflect back, I see that I had been preparing my whole life for a role that would allow broad impact on others early on in my career. Having a moldable heart and mind has shaped my experiences along the way. I learned that we tend to create precise roadmaps for our lives. But, we must give ourselves the liberty to fail, take detours and risks, and learn to be flexible. Trusting that things will fall into place to serve the greater purpose is the best choice. It allows us to smell the flowers and enjoy the journey.

We must listen to our inner intuition that stems from our core values and let it pave the right road towards a greater plan. This has helped me approach adversity with curiosity and seek the lessons to be learned. I know that as a child of God or a Higher Being, I will never be presented with something I can't overcome.

# I Love You, Body

*I love you, body,*
      *Yes I do!*
*Your curves and stretch marks*
   *And scars from my wounds and joy from my journey,*
      *Long with ups and downs,*
         *Light and darkness,*
            *You, my body, with strength abound!*

*You carry my spirit, my sadness and joy,*
   *Every single decision I make or don't.*
*My body,*
   *Temple and vessel of the Divine,*
      *Made of the same stuff of stars,*
         *The combination of what you are made of,*
            *In perfect proportion to that of Mother Earth,*
*My body,*
*I love you, I do!*

*I work you out,*
*I put you in shape,*
*But what I really want is to fully embrace*
   *And accept you,*
      *My body,*
         *Made of the same stuff of stars,*
            *Temple and vessel of the Divine.*

# What can I do today to make this the best year of my life?

_____

_____

_____

_____

_____

_____

# You, the Star

*Stardust—*
    *It's what we are made of.*
*The stars—*
*Our original home.*
    *To shine—*
        *Our most natural capacity and birthright.*

*In your own beautiful way,*
    *Like the star in our perceived sky,*
        *You shine,*
            *And when you do,*
                *I shine, too.*
*Let's shine for all of us—*
        *Bright!*
            *Like the star that you, I, we are!*

# What can I do today to make this the best year of my life?

_____
_____
_____
_____
_____
_____
_____

# A Poem for Change

*Funny it seems,*
*That we ask for things and we get them.*
*Oh yes, we get these things we ask for, indeed . . .*
*Through change we get these things we ask for.*
*Why not accept the things we have been asking for?*
*Accept, receive, let go, forgive,*
*And say thank you some more . . .*
*Thank you, God,*
*Universe, all powerful power that is all . . .*
*Thank you for giving us all that we ask for.*

# What can I do today to make this the best year of my life?

_____

_____

_____

_____

_____

_____

_____

# Capable and Worthy

*You are capable, courageous.*
*You are cared for and divinely protected.*
*You are strong and magnetic.*
*You can do this and so much more!*
*You will when you act with clear intent.*
*Your intentions are powerful, like you.*
*You are very powerful.*
*You are the power.*
*You are success and beyond.*
*You are successful.*
*You are creative, worthy and totally capable.*
*You are whatever you want to be.*
*You are whatever you set your mind to be—*
*heart, spirit and body to be!*
*You are capable and worthy.*
*Take the step.*
*You'll see how strong you can be!*

# What can I do today to make this the best year of my life?

_____

_____

_____

_____

_____

_____

# Bonus Material

## The Ten-Ten-Ten®
## Reading/Study Skills System

*"There are three ingredients in the good life:*
*learning, earning and yearning."*
—Christopher Morley

It was my dear teacher, friend and mentor Hassan Antar, who through a series of phone conversations shared with me this model of efficient learning he developed through working with thousands of students in his career as an educator, artist, Marshall arts master, father and devoted friend.

He mailed over to me a package which contained the details of the 10-10-10 learning system. In my last conversation with him while he lived in New Mexico in 2014, he told me to share this knowledge in the spirit of helping anyone who desires to learn anything have a more gentle and efficient way to learn. I share this information with you in his honor.

The Ten-Ten-Ten® Reading/Study Technique is a proven system for enhancing your retention and comprehension of information. To achieve your goals and create your best year ever, it will be necessary to expand your knowledge base: the information that you've been exposed to and the insights that you have about your world. Reading enables you do that.

While you might be doing a lot of seeking and reading to find answers and gain insights, it's important to know that the majority of people forget 50% of whatever they read within twenty-four hours, and forget 75% of what they read within forty-eight hours.

As with most things in life, this system is most effective when practiced over a period of time, and when used systematically for successive tasks. Using it consistently and correctly will help build and strengthen the disciplines and focus necessary for your success. It is an efficient method of developing comprehension skills for students of all ages. It has also been widely acclaimed by people involved in independent research testing its impact on knowledge retention. It is also useful for anyone who simply wishes to retain any particular information.

**Method:** The 10-10-10® is divided into three segments as follows:

**1.** For the first segment, find a quiet place to sit, and using a timer, take ten minutes to read or study silently the given text. Don't let anything or anyone distract your concentration or alter your focus. If the material is short and you finish reading before the ten minutes are up, simply begin again, re-reading and reviewing it. At the end of the ten minutes, take a three-minute break.

**2.** In the second segment, the same rules apply—however this time you read aloud, in your regular speaking voice. Speaking aloud engages your subconscious mind and allows the content to become more deeply rooted in your brain. At the end of the ten minutes, again take a three-minute break.

**3.** During the last segment, quiz yourself aloud, or have a partner quiz you. The questions posed should be those that produce a compound response: that is, no simple yes or no answers. Don't simply parrot the information back, but use your thinking process to come up with answers that reflect your unique thoughts or feelings on the subject. This helps you to master what you have just read.

# Be the Gift

You are a gifted creator, maker,
be-er, live-er, writer, artist
And speaker of truths,
A channel: you are a goddess of truth,
Wise, wise, wise—so wise!
Deep breath! Inhale, exhale.
Relax, accept the amazing being that you are.
Give the best of what you have.
Receive, for you have asked and also given.
Continue, stop and rest.
Go on and relax some more.
You already are what you want, what you are,
You, you gifted creator of your reality, you are!
Deep breaths and a smiling peaceful inner state
And outer space, plus a joyful heart
At all times.
Remember always all the good that you have,
Right now.
Not that you don't care about what may need changing,
It's that you choose to rest into peace
And God,
As you, the gift!

# What can I do today to make this the best year of my life?

_____

_____

_____

_____

_____

_____

_____

# What can I do today to make this the best year of my life?

_____

_____

_____

_____

_____

_____

_____

# Our Established Worth

*Your worth, established before conception,*
*Merely lost by distorted perception,*
*The illusion of separation,*
*A forgotten validation.*
*The game of experience is to*
*Return to the perception.*
*That perfection*
*Is never lost,*
*Even through the bad translation*
*Of life's rejections.*
*You can go back, make it right;*
*The game is expansion.*
*You can crack the code and build and live*
*In a heavenly playground.*
*Heaven is where you will live,*
*Here on Earth, inside and out.*
*When you remember your truth, your worth,*
*You'll see!*

Let the universe hear what
you want this year!

# Acknowledgments

*It truly takes a village to raise anything important. I am thankful for this opportunity to thank my village.*

*The Source, God, from which everything derives, has endowed me worthy of being an instrument of good. May my life and experiences uplift those I come into contact with, always.*

*My partner Chris and my daughter Angelina keep me real and true. I can't ask for more love than that.*

*My mother Digna and my siblings, Gina, Andria and Eddy—your never-ending support allows me to be free of worry. I am thankful for the way you and my entire family see me as someone you can count on. I love you all. It was with you all in my heart that I wrote this book.*

*My angel of an editor Ellen Keiter was a gift from the Divine.*

*My thought partner and amiga Linda—the way we hold space for each other's intentions each week truly moved me in the direction of seeing this book come to life.*

*And to my other amigas in life who listen, support, trust and share their life with me—Massiel, Rosa, Ivanna, Sheggai, Latonia, and so many others—you inspire me in more ways than you know.*

*A deep, deep, deep bow to my coaching clients who have been some of my greatest teachers. My heart is more open and fulfilled because of you.*

*Thank you. Gratitude. Muchas gracias.*

# About the Author

**Clara Angelina Diaz** declares her superpower to be her keen intuitive ability to connect the dots and find solutions quickly.

Completely bilingual and a proud immigrant from The Dominican Republic, Clara is a certified master-level life and business success coach, speaker, artist, and author. Most importantly, she is a mother, and is the eldest of six children.

In her coaching practice she supports powerful women and organizations who love them. Her audiobook and self-coaching program, *Create Your Best Year (One Day at a Time),* available in both English in Spanish, is revolutionizing the way women focus their energy and own their gifts.

Clara is the recipient of the Inspirational Leadership and Community Empowerment Award for her leadership development work with the women of Brockton, Massachusetts, and is a regular mentor for the Center for Women and Enterprise Women's Leadership Conference and Entrepreneurship for All's Spanish program, *Negocios Exitosos* (Successful Businesses). She has a self-designed degree from Lesley University in Life and Business Management, and a certification in Life and Business Coaching from Wainwright International School of Coaching. She lives in Massachusetts with her daughter and partner.

Printed in the United States
By Bookmasters